DRAW RAINFOREST Animals

by Doug DuBosque

PEEL productions, inc.

Cataloging-in-Publication Data

DuBosque, D. C.
        Draw rainforest animals / by Doug DuBosque
            p. cm.
        Includes index.
        ISBN 0-939217-23-6 : $8.95

        1. Rain forest fauna in art--Juvenile literature. 2.
Drawing--Technique--Juvenile literature. [1. Rain forest
animals in art. 2. Drawing--Technique.] I. Title.

743'.6   94-69427

Distributed to the trade and art
markets in North America by

NORTH LIGHT BOOKS,
an imprint of F&W Publications, Inc.
4700 East Galbraith Road
Cincinnati, OH 45236

(800) 289-0963

Contents

Basilisk Lizard 6

Chimpanzee 8

Emerald Tree Boa 10

Flying Squirrel 12

Frog 1 (Arrow Poison) 14

Frog 2 (Flying) 15

Frog 3 (Tree) 16

Gorilla 18

Hoatzin 20

Howler Monkey 22

Iguana 24

Jaguar 26

Kinkajou 28

Ruffed Lemur 30

Macaw 32

Margay 34

Okapi 36

Orangutan 38

Ouakari 40

Pangolin 42

Quetzal 44

Slender Loris 46

Sloth 48

Spider Monkey 50

Tamandua 52

Tapir 54

Toucan 56

Vine Snake 58

Other Ideas & Drawing Tips 60

Index 63

 # A few thoughts before you start...

Rainforests - cool!

The rainforests, or jungles, of the world hold plenty of surprises for those who explore them. Let's do that with a pencil!

Draw Rainforest Animals shows you how to draw fascinating creatures, step by step. You may find some of them quite easy. Others present more challenges.

What do you need?

- **pencil**
  (2B or 3B will work well)
- **pencil sharpener**
- **eraser**
  (kneadable works best)
- **paper**
  (test of quality: how easily can you erase on it?)
- **place to draw**
  Good light, no distractions.

And don't forget...

- **positive attitude**
  Forget *"I can't."*
  Say, *"I'm learning."*

You drawings may not be perfect the first time. Keep working on them!

Think of drawing in three stages.

First

Read the instructions. LOOK carefully at the animal you wish to draw! See the shapes and pieces and how they fit together.

Then, lightly sketch the shapes in the right place.

When you sketch lightly, you can easily correct any mistakes before they ruin your drawing.

Second

Once you have the basic shapes and lines right,
- add more complicated parts,
- add shading,
- add detail, and
- erase lines you no longer need.

Third

Make your drawing jump off the page!
- add more shading,
- sharpen details,
- clean up with your eraser, and
- date and save your drawing in a portfolio *(see p.62).*

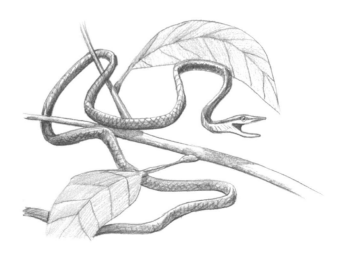

Just so you know...

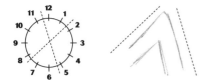

Clock faces appear from time to time. Use them as a reference to see the tilt of ovals, legs, and other angles in the drawing.

And now, let's

Look signs point out visual elements of the drawing – in this example, a curve turns almost vertical.

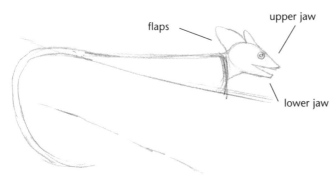

flaps   upper jaw

lower jaw

Labels will help you identify the parts of the animal mentioned in the text.

Basilisk Lizard

Always draw lightly at first!

Basiliscus plumifrons: South America. Size: 80 cm (31 inches). Feeds on fruit and small animals during the day. Few four-legged animals can run on two legs the way this lizard does. It can even run a short distance across water!

1. Start with two slanting lines for the branch. Lightly draw a long triangle for the lizard's body. Add the long, curving tail.

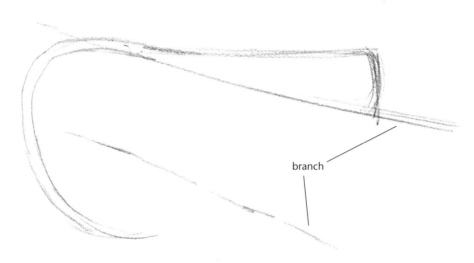

branch

2. Still drawing very lightly, make an oval for the head. Add the upper and lower jaws at one end. Draw the neck and flaps on top of the head. Carefully place the eye, above the back of the mouth.

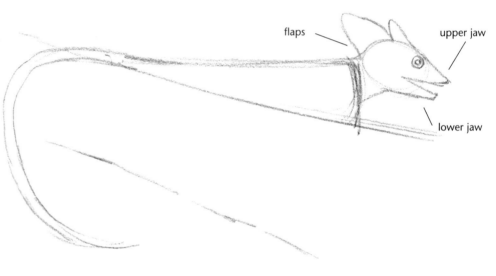

flaps

upper jaw

lower jaw

3. Look closely at the legs grabbing the branch. Draw the legs – one piece at a time.

Draw lightly at first!

Sit back, take a deep breath, and really look at your drawing. Do all the proportions look correct? Is there anything you need to improve before continuing?

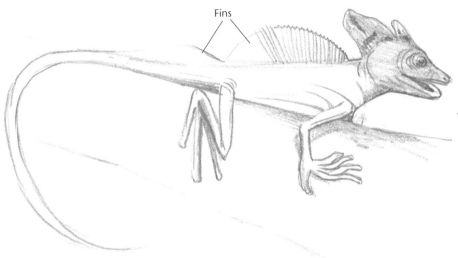

Fins

4. Lightly outline the fins on the back. Sharpen your pencil to put the fine lines inside them, and give them jagged edges. Add wrinkles on the face and body. As you pencil gets dull, start to add shading.

cast shadow

5. Shade slowly and carefully, using the side of your pencil if you find it helpful. Add stripes to the tail, and a cast shadow underneath. Use rough pencil marks to show texture.

6. With a sharpened pencil, go over lines, darkening and adding emphasis. As your pencil gets dull, do more shading. Finally, clean up any smudges with your eraser.

Chimpanzee

Pan troglodytes: Africa. Intelligent and expressive animals, chimpanzees spend most of their time on the ground, walking on all fours and occasionally standing erect. They are good climbers. They eat plant materials, plus insects and eggs – they even use tools like twigs to extract ants or termites!

1. In this drawing, the face is important, so take time to get it right! Draw two light circles, with a tall oval touching the bottom of both.

2. Near the bottom of the lower oval, draw a line for the mouth. At the top of the oval, draw two nostrils with heart-shaped outline. Add curved lines for eyes.

3. Draw the lower lip. what other details do you see? Add them!

4. Add radiating lines to complete the head. Add ears.

5. Lightly draw two overlapping ovals for the body. Which is higher? Which is bigger? Which is flatter?

6. Look at the back legs. Which lines go straight up and down (vertical)? Where does each leg start? Which direction does it go? Now draw them – very lightly until you've got them just right.

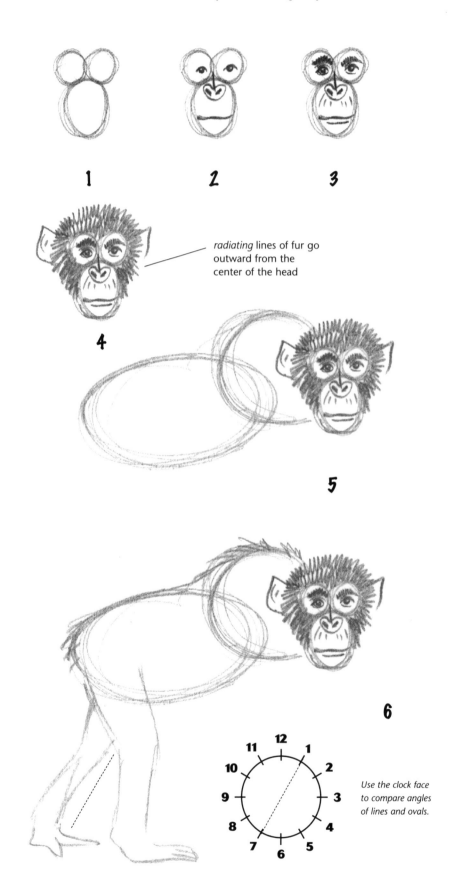

1

2

3

radiating lines of fur go outward from the center of the head

4

5

6

Use the clock face to compare angles of lines and ovals.

7. Lightly draw the arms. (If it helps you, add a line for the ground.) Look carefully at the shape of the arms and hands.

   Make short pencil guide lines showing the direction of the fur.

cast shadow

8. Following those guide lines, add fur to the body. Look how the ovals disappear – no need to erase! Add a slight cast shadow on the ground.

 Turn your drawing as you draw to avoid smudging it with your hand.

Sit back, take a deep breath and really look at your drawing (perhaps in a mirror). Does it need darker fur? Sharper details on the face or hands? If so, do them now.

Clean up any smudges with your eraser.

Pssssst…if nobody's listening, make some chimp sounds….

Emerald Tree Boa

Boa caninus: South America
Size: 1.2 m (4 ft). Brilliant green
snake with prehensile tail spends its
life in trees, where it lies in wait for
prey, often birds and bats. Fast, and
a good swimmer.

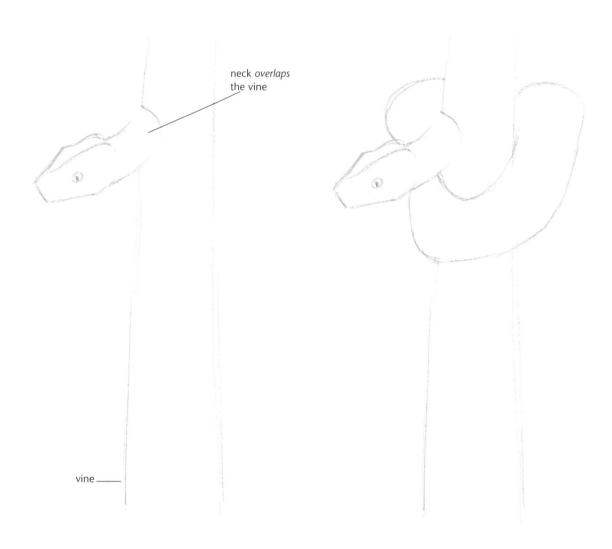

neck *overlaps*
the vine

vine _____

Be creative! Draw this snake in different positions. You don't have to follow my drawing exactly!

1. Start with two light *vertical* lines for the vine. Draw the head with eye, and the first section of the body, *overlapping* part of the vine.

   Make the front of the head blunt. Each eyebrow bulges slightly.

2. Add the next section of the body, forming a rough U shape.

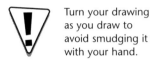

Turn your drawing as you draw to avoid smudging it with your hand.

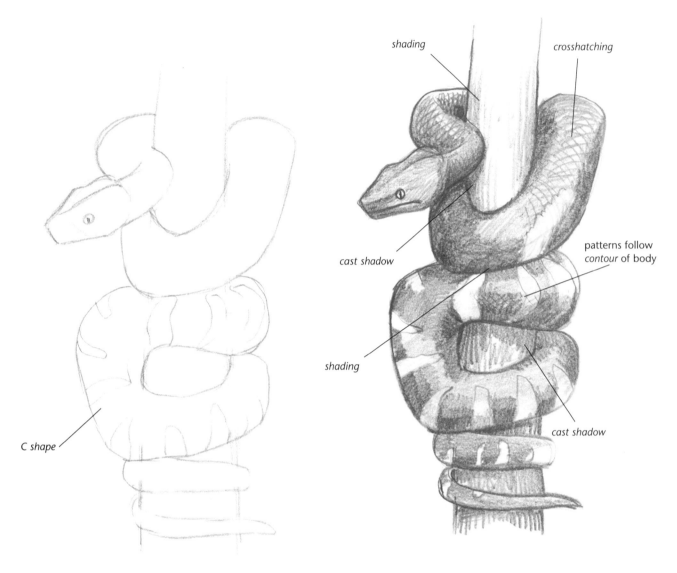

shading

crosshatching

cast shadow

patterns follow contour of body

shading

cast shadow

C shape

3. Below the U shape, make another section of the body, this time a fat C shape. Add a couple more sections, getting smaller and smaller....

   Notice that the snake doesn't wrap around the vine in one continuous spiral. The tail wraps all the way around, but the larger parts of the body reverse direction to form 'clamps' to hold to the vine.

4. Now try to make the snake and vine look round.

   Look carefully for:
   • the pattern of curving white spots,
   • crosshatching to suggest scales,
   • shading on the snake and the vine, and
   • cast shadows on the vine and snake.

   You're on your own! Keep shading until it looks like it's ready to jump off the page!

   Good looking boa!

Flying Squirrel

Anomalurus beecrofti (Beecroft's flying squirrel): West and central Africa. Size: 53-84 cm (20-33 inches) overall length. Lives in trees. Feeds mostly on berries, seeds and fruit. Glides up to 90 m (300 ft) from tree to tree.

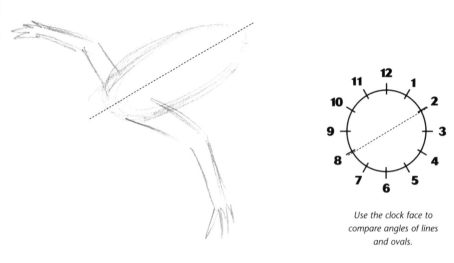

1. Draw a tilted oval, with two extended front legs. Make them bend slightly.

Use the clock face to compare angles of lines and ovals.

2. Add the rear legs, with two bends (knee and ankle).

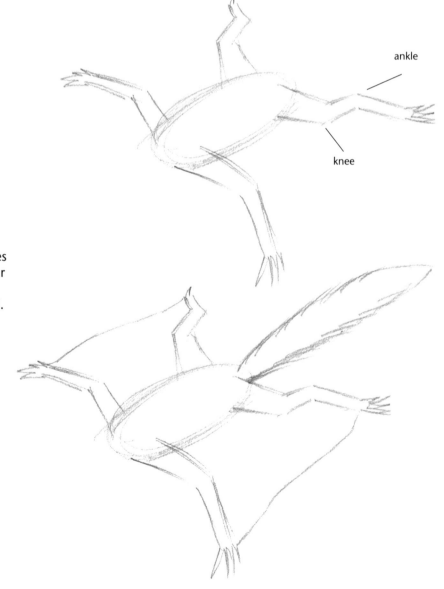

ankle

knee

3. Draw slightly curved lines to connect front and rear feet. Use short pencil strokes for the bushy tail.

4. Draw an oval for the head, slightly pointed at the nose. Add the eye and ears.

5. Draw the fur, using short pencil strokes. Leave some areas white. Add detail to the eye. Draw whiskers. Sharpen details. Clean up any smudges with your eraser.

Idea: add some leaves behind the squirrel. Draw the branch the squirrel just launched from.

Frog 1 (Arrow Poison)

Dendrobates auratus: Central and South America. Size: 4 cm (1.5 inches). Bright red coloring warns predators that this frog is poisonous! Local tribesman know how to extract the poison, which they use on the tips of hunting arrows.

1. Draw two overlapping ovals. Draw them very lightly! You'll see why in a moment.

2. Add a bump for the hip, a bump at the top of the head, a bump for the nose, and one more for the throat. Erase the ovals where they overlap. Draw a circle for the eye – leave a small white spot when you darken it. Add the curving lines for the top and bottom of the eye.

3. Add the legs. Look where and how each leg attaches to the body, and the angles of each segment of the legs. Erase the oval where the leg overlaps it.

4. As your pencil gets dull, add shading. Leave part of the back very light to help make it look shiny. When you sharpen your pencil, go over details and outlines to make them sharper.

   Add the cast shadow under the frog. Clean up any smudges with your eraser.

   If you want to use color, make the frog bright orange with black spots.

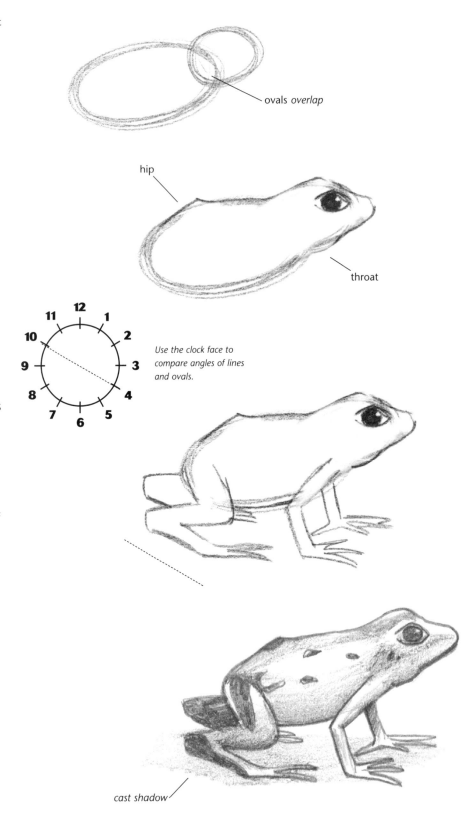

ovals *overlap*

hip

throat

Use the clock face to compare angles of lines and ovals.

cast shadow

Frog 2 (Flying)

Rhacophorus nigropalmatus (Wallace's flying frog): Southeast Asia. This 10-cm (4-inch) long frog glides from tree to tree. The webs and skin flaps act like a parachute.

1. Draw a tall, narrow triangle for the body. Add two L-shaped arms to it.

2. Add bumps on the triangle for the nose and eyes. Draw four fingers to each arm. Connect the ends of the fingers to make the webs. Draw Z-shaped legs.

3. Add toes and webbing to the legs. Draw curves in the arms and legs.

4. Shade the dark, webbed parts of the feet. Add shading to the rest of the frog.

   Clean up any smudges with your eraser.

Idea: you're looking down on a frog gliding high above the ground. What would it see below it? Can you draw that?

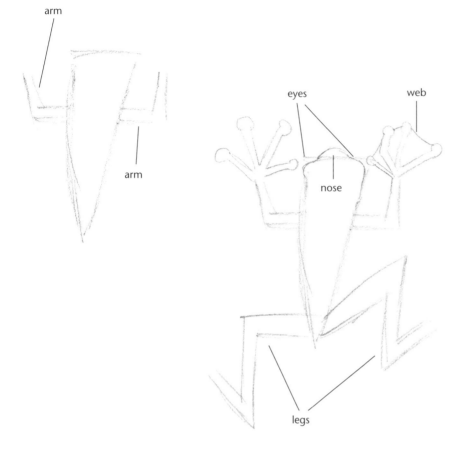

arm

arm

eyes

web

nose

legs

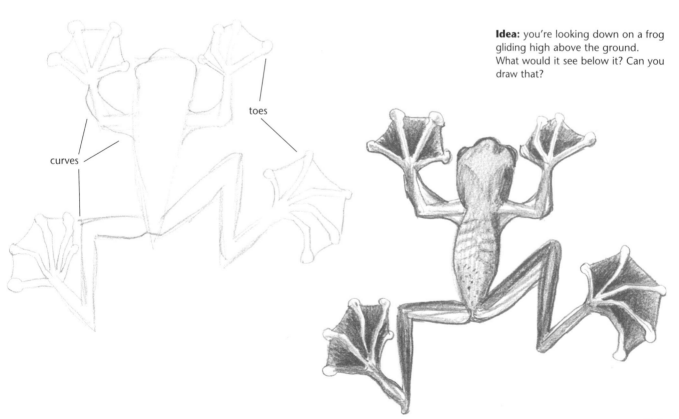

curves

toes

Frog 3 (Tree)

Phyllomedusa appendiculata (Lutz's Phyllomedusa): Southeast Brazil. Size: 4 cm (1.5 inches). Lives in trees, feeds on insects. Lays eggs in a protective leaf over water. When the tadpoles hatch, they fall into the water.

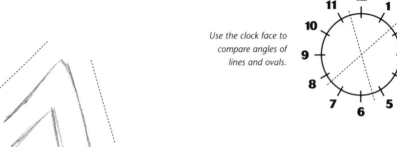

Use the clock face to compare angles of lines and ovals.

In this view, you don't see the whole frog. Look at the final drawing. See how many parts of the body *overlap*.

1. Start with 2 upside-down V shapes for the front leg.

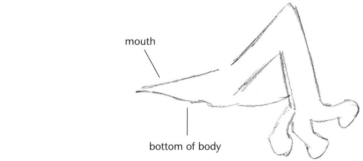

mouth

bottom of body

2. Add three fingers. Draw a curving line for the bottom part of the body, then a straight line for the mouth.

rear toes

3. Add two sideways V shapes for the other front leg. Draw the rear toes.

other front leg

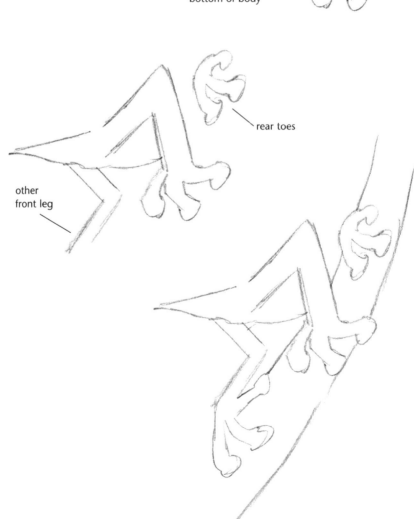

4. Draw toes for the other front leg, then carefully draw curving lines for the branch.

   With so many toes overlapping *the branch, it's easier to draw them first, then add the branch behind.*

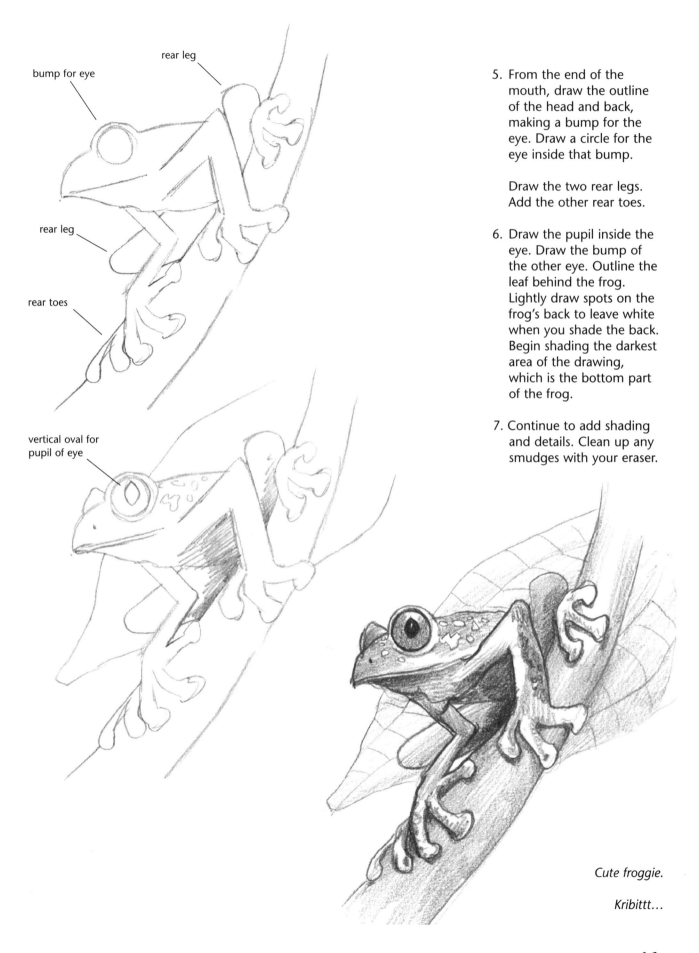

bump for eye

rear leg

rear leg

rear toes

vertical oval for
pupil of eye

5. From the end of the
   mouth, draw the outline
   of the head and back,
   making a bump for the
   eye. Draw a circle for the
   eye inside that bump.

   Draw the two rear legs.
   Add the other rear toes.

6. Draw the pupil inside the
   eye. Draw the bump of
   the other eye. Outline the
   leaf behind the frog.
   Lightly draw spots on the
   frog's back to leave white
   when you shade the back.
   Begin shading the darkest
   area of the drawing,
   which is the bottom part
   of the frog.

7. Continue to add shading
   and details. Clean up any
   smudges with your eraser.

Cute froggie.

Kribittt…

Gorilla

Gorilla gorilla: Africa, in rain forests to fairly high elevations. Size: male height 1.7-1.8 m (5.5-6 ft); female height 1.4-1.5 m (4.5-5 ft). Largest of the primates, gorillas are gentle animals unless threatened. They eat mainly plants. They live in small groups. *Easy scientific name!*

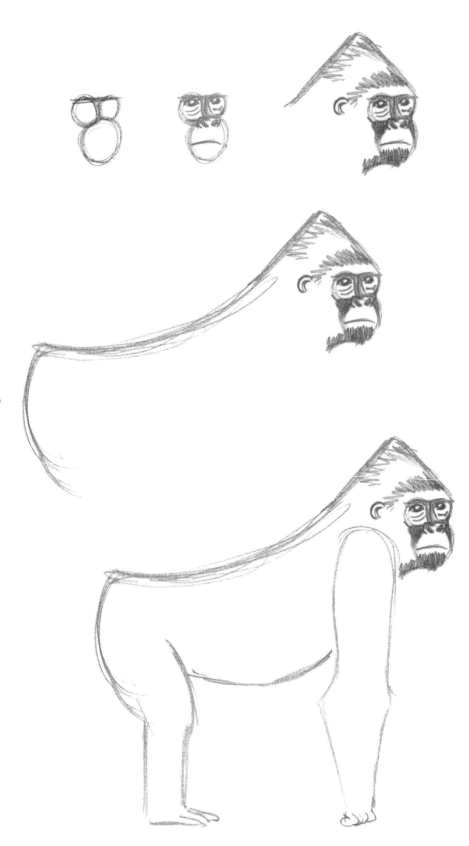

1. Draw two small circles on top of a larger oval. Make a line across them to help emphasize the strong brow of the gorilla.

2. Draw a line for the mouth. Add eyes, with lines under them. Draw slanting nostrils.

3. From the edge of the eyebrow, draw a line up to a point and back down – like a pyramid on the gorilla's head. This part of the head is almost as high as the face! Add the ear, and short pencil lines on the chin, face and forehead.

4. From the back of the head, make a long swooping line for the back, joined by another swooping line for the back of the leg.

5. Lightly draw the leg and arm, with toes and fingers. Notice the shape of the arm. Look how close the shoulder comes to the face.

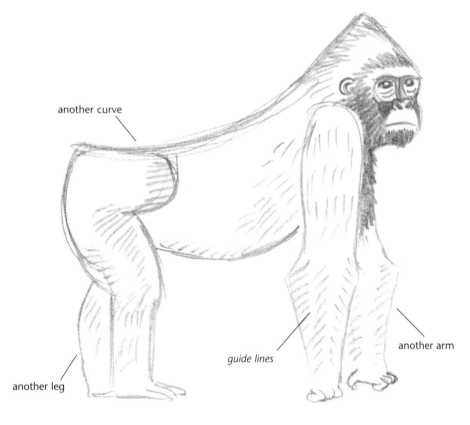

another curve

guide lines

another arm

another leg

6. Add the other leg and arm. Before you add fur, make light *guide lines* to remind you which direction the shading needs to go.

7. Cover the whole body with short pencil strokes. Be sure to follow the direction of your *guide lines*.

Pay attention to areas that are lighter and darker. Go over lines that need to be darker or sharper, and refine details of the face if you need to.

Which areas are lightest? Which areas are darkest?

Add a cast shadow underneath.

cast shadow

Bright idea: if a gorilla charges you in the wild, *stand your ground.* If you run, you'll be in big trouble.

Hoatzin

Opisthocomus hoazin: South America. Size: 61 cm (24 inches). Bizarre bird lives in trees, and doesn't fly well. Eats fruit and leaves. Young can swim, and have claws on the hook of each wing to help them climb trees…nests are built over water so they can drop to safety if a snake approaches!

1. Draw a tilted oval. At the top, add a curve like an upside-down smile. This will become the top of the head.

2. From the top of the head, draw the neck and breast. Add the mouth, and the eye.

   Lightly draw curved lines to show where the first three layers of wing feathers end. The longest feathers extend beyond the oval. Draw the outline of the wing, then add light lines for the feathers.

3. Draw the wild feathers sticking out the top of the head. Outline the eye and beak and light feathers running down the neck. Darken the top of the head. 'Ruffle' the breast feathers with short pencil strokes.

   Add feathers on the back. Outline a small space at the end of each layer of feathers on the wing – leave this area white. Add points on the end of the longest feathers.

Use the clock face to compare angles of lines and ovals.

Tail feathers

4. Add a tree branch, with the bird's claws. Lightly draw the tail feathers.

5. Take a moment to look at the final drawing, noticing white and dark areas. Add shading. Finish the tail feathers, leaving the ends white.

! Turn your drawing as you draw to avoid smudging it with your hand.

Handsome hoatzin!

Howler Monkey

Alouatta seniculus (red howler monkey): northern South America, mainly Colombia. Size: 160-180 cm (63-71 inches). Lives in trees, eats leaves and some fruit. Sturdily built, with prehensile tail. They're loud! Male howler monkeys shout to let other monkeys know their territory.

Use the clock face to compare angles of lines and ovals.

1. Start by drawing three overlapping ovals. Notice how each tilts at a different angle.

2. Draw the face, one feature at a time, starting with the mouth.

3. Add the outline of the head, and join the ovals to make the curved back. Draw the arm and leg on the side closest to you – pay attention to the way they bend. Add fur to the chin.

4. Draw the remaining arm and leg, and the tail. As you draw them, add branches. Notice how the tail curls around one branch.

5. Use your eraser to clean up lines you won't need in the finished drawing. Starting with the darkest areas, make short pencil lines for fur.

6. Look carefully at which parts of the monkey are darkest, and which are lightest. Continue adding fur. Draw shading on the branches.

While your pencil is sharp, go over fine details. As it gets duller, add shading.

 Turn your drawing as you draw to avoid smudging it with your hand.

Clean up any smudges with your eraser.

Iguana

Iguana iguana (common iguana): Central and South America.
Size: 1-2 m (3.5-6.5 ft). Iguanas live in trees, but lay eggs in holes they dig in the ground. They feed on plants, but can defend themselves from other animals with sharp teeth and claws. They drop from trees into water to escape – they're great swimmers! *Easy scientific name!*

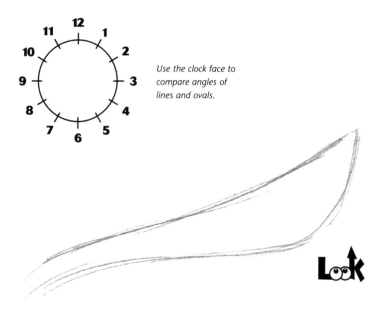

Use the clock face to compare angles of lines and ovals.

1. Begin with the swooping shape for the body. Notice how the bottom line becomes almost vertical at the head. Don't join the lines at the tail yet – it gets a lot longer!

foreshortening makes the leg look like it's coming toward you

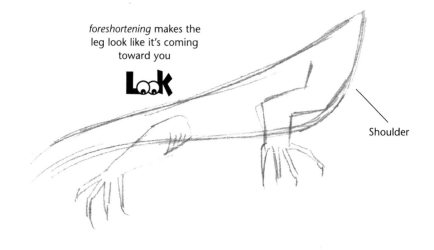

Shoulder

2. Look at the legs. The front leg starts at the shoulder, goes down, back, then down again. The back leg is foreshortened. This means that part of it (the part connecting to the body) comes straight towards you. Now draw the legs, and add toes and claws.

Spikes

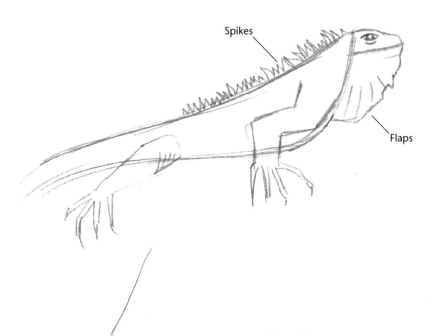

Flaps

3. Add the top of the head, and eye. Draw a line for the mouth, then add the flaps of skin beneath the mouth. Add the distinct, jagged row of spikes along the iguana's back. They don't need to be even.

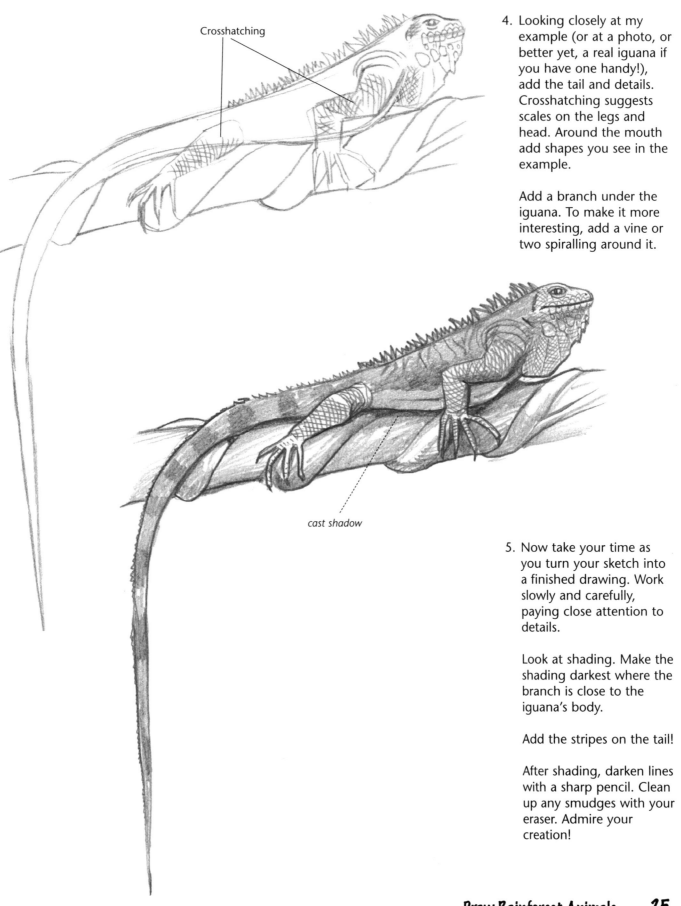

Crosshatching

cast shadow

4. Looking closely at my example (or at a photo, or better yet, a real iguana if you have one handy!), add the tail and details. Crosshatching suggests scales on the legs and head. Around the mouth add shapes you see in the example.

Add a branch under the iguana. To make it more interesting, add a vine or two spiralling around it.

5. Now take your time as you turn your sketch into a finished drawing. Work slowly and carefully, paying close attention to details.

Look at shading. Make the shading darkest where the branch is close to the iguana's body.

Add the stripes on the tail!

After shading, darken lines with a sharp pencil. Clean up any smudges with your eraser. Admire your creation!

Jaguar

Panthera onca: Central and South America. Size: 1.5-1.8 m ((5-6 ft). Climbs trees to lie in wait for prey. Feeds on a variety of animals, even fish. Powerful animal with deep chest and strong limbs.

1. Start by drawing two light, *overlapping* circles.

2. Add the two sides of the mouth slanting downward, with the small vertical line in the center.

3. Add a flat triangle for the nose.

4. Directly above the outside of the nose, draw two upside-down L shapes.

5. Make eyes by drawing curves down from the outside of the L shapes. Add ears.

6. Make a circle for the center of the eye – leave a small highlight in it.

7. Darken the rest of each eye. Add rows of dots on the muzzle and whiskers.

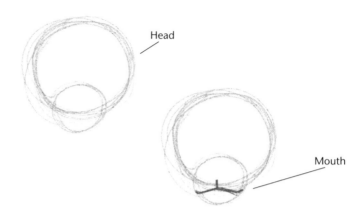

Head

Mouth

The secret to drawing the jaguar – or other cats – is getting the face right. Rather than trying to draw this perfectly the first time, try it several times on scratch paper. Draw a little larger than you normally do. Pay attention to proportions.

When you have the face mastered, look ahead to steps 8-10. Leave enough room on your paper for the body!

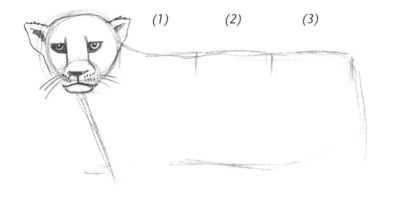

(1)   (2)   (3)

8. Measure three heads back for the length of the body. Make the back level with the bottom of the eyes, with a little curve at the neck. Make the front of the body slant slightly.

9. Add the legs and paws. *Draw lightly at first.* Look at your jaguar. Is everything the way you want it?

If something looks wrong, try looking at your picture in a mirror, or hold it up to a light and look through the back.

10. Next add spots to the jaguar – dark patches, with one or more darker spots inside. These large spots become smaller spots and stripes on the legs and tail.

Lightly lay out the pattern, then carefully add shading. It takes a while, but it's worth it!

While your pencil is sharp, go over fine details. As it gets duller, add shading.

 Turn your drawing as you draw to avoid smudging it with your hand.

Clean up any smudges with your eraser.

Here, kitty…nice kitty…

Kinkajou

Potos flavus: Central and South America. Size: 81-113 cm (32-45 inches). Kinkajous live in trees, feeding at night on fruit and insects. Agile climbers, they use their prehensile tail to hold onto branches, leaving their hands free for gathering food.

1. Start by drawing downward-curving lines for the branch, and a titled oval. The angle of the branch helps emphasize the kinkajou's prehensile tail in this drawing.

Head

2. Lightly draw an oval for the upper body and a small circle for the head.

overlapping

LooK

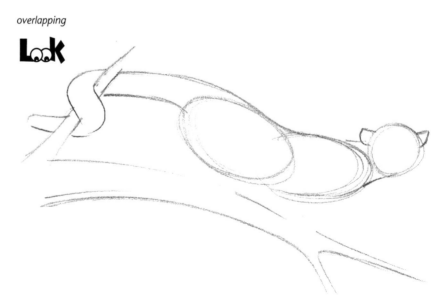

3. Add another small branch behind the animal, and draw the tail curling around it (look closely at my example to see how to do this!). Add ears and the outline of the back and neck.

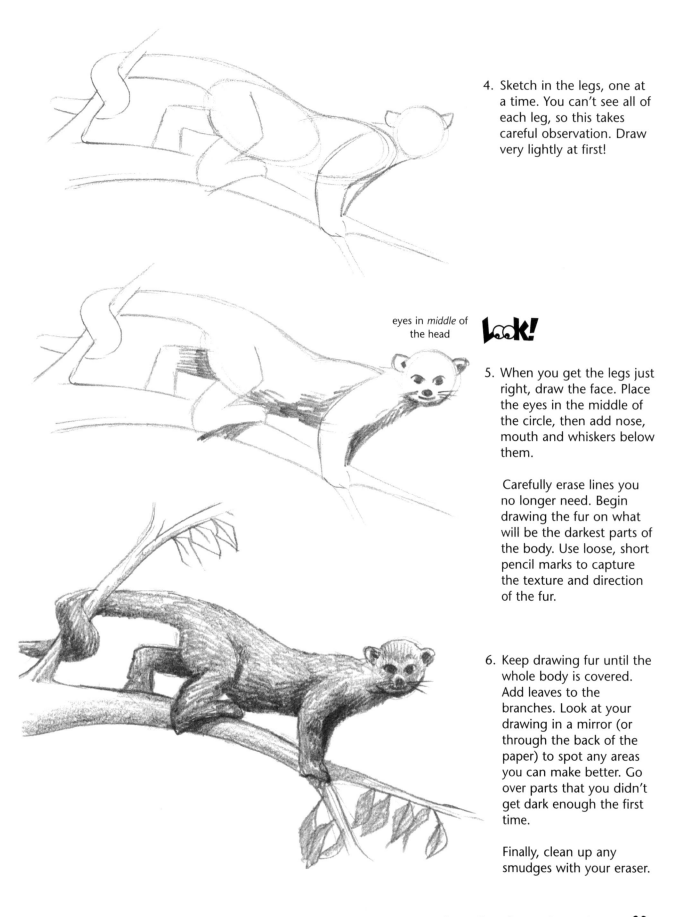

4. Sketch in the legs, one at a time. You can't see all of each leg, so this takes careful observation. Draw very lightly at first!

eyes in *middle* of the head

Look!

5. When you get the legs just right, draw the face. Place the eyes in the middle of the circle, then add nose, mouth and whiskers below them.

Carefully erase lines you no longer need. Begin drawing the fur on what will be the darkest parts of the body. Use loose, short pencil marks to capture the texture and direction of the fur.

6. Keep drawing fur until the whole body is covered. Add leaves to the branches. Look at your drawing in a mirror (or through the back of the paper) to spot any areas you can make better. Go over parts that you didn't get dark enough the first time.

Finally, clean up any smudges with your eraser.

Ruffed Lemur

Varecia variegata: Madagascar.
Size: 120 cm (47 inches) including
tail. This agile climber rarely comes
to the ground. It eats fruit, leaves
and bark, and is most active at dusk
and the early part of the night.

1. Start with the eyes: small
   circles with a spot inside
   them, surrounded by
   wider, darker circles.

2. Draw the outline of the
   head, a rectangle above
   the eyes and a rounded
   triangle below the eyes.

3. Add the nose and mouth.

4. From the top sides of the
   head, lightly draw lines
   going out and up. Then
   draw the outline of the
   curving ruff, or collar, or
   beard, or whatever you
   want to call it.

   Draw lightly at first!

   Once you have the light
   outline in place, add
   radiating lines for the fur.

Ruff

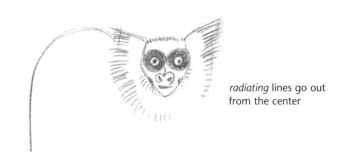

radiating lines go out
from the center

5. Draw a light curving line
   for the back. Continue
   adding lines for fur around
   the face.

6. Draw the curve of the leg.
   *What number does this look
   like?* Add five radiating
   curved lines for the toes.

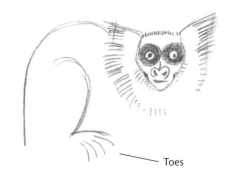

Toes

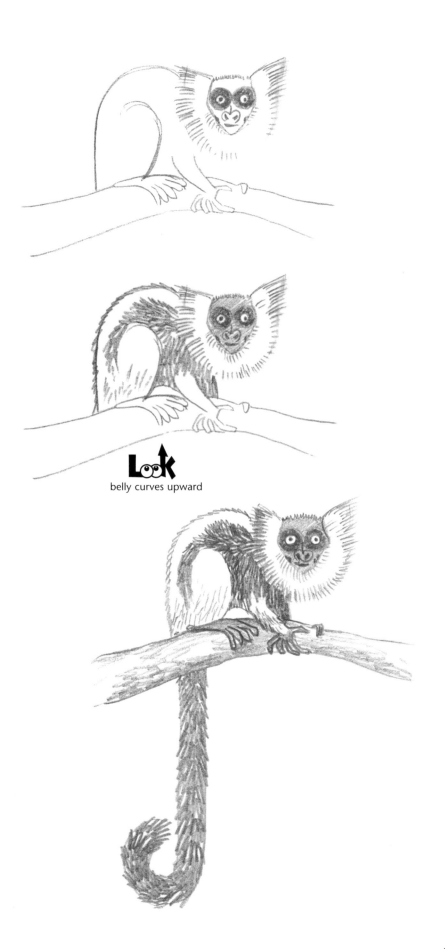

belly curves upward

7. Complete the rear foot. Draw the front arm and hand, with all five fingers. Draw the lines of the branch, adding a tiny bit of the thumb of the other hand.

8. Add a small upward curve for the lemur's belly, and the dark fur of the other arm. With short pencil strokes radiating from the shoulder, draw more fur. Add jagged lines along the back for texture, and a few fur lines on the face and body.

   What's missing?

9. A fat, long tail! Try drawing it using only short lines for the fur.

   While your pencil is sharp, go over fine details. As it gets duller, add shading.

    Turn your drawing as you draw to avoid smudging it with your hand.

   Clean up any smudges with your eraser.

   Idea: add leaves and other branches in the background. Draw a dark background to make a night setting for this nocturnal animal.

Macaw

Ara macao (Scarlet macaw): Mexico to northern South America. Size: 85 cm (33.5 inches). Most familiar of South American parrots. Threatened by destruction of rain forest and people stealing baby birds to sell as pets. Don't buy them!

1. Lightly draw the top part of the beak, then the bottom.

2. Add a roughly triangular shape for the macaw's face. At the top of it, draw the eye. Add the pattern of spots on the cheek, and a few curved lines to suggest the texture of the beak.

3. From the top of the beak, draw the outline of the macaw's head. From the bottom of the beak, draw the throat. Connect front and back with a shoulder line.

4. LIghtly draw an oval for the bird's body. Draw two claws grasping a branch.

5. Sketch in the tail feathers. Notice that they stick out a bit, rather than pointing straight down.

Top of beak

Bottom of beak

Use the clock face to compare angles of lines and ovals.

Head

Shoulder

shoulder line

Claws

Tail feathers

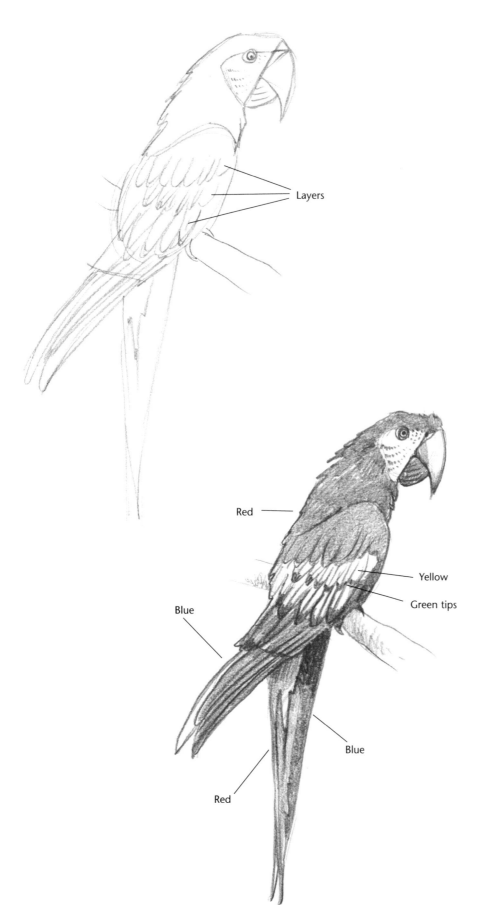

Layers

6. Add lines to these wing feathers, then draw the tail feathers, pointing downward underneath the wing feathers. Add three layers of feathers on the wing.

7. Carefully shade the feathers. While your pencil is sharp, go over fine details. As it gets duller, add shading.

 Turn your drawing as you draw to avoid smudging it with your hand.

Look at your drawing in a mirror (or through the back of the paper) to spot any areas you can make better.

Clean up any smudges with your eraser.

Red

Blue

Red

Yellow

Green tips

Blue

Idea: draw it in color!

Margay

Felis Wiedii: Central and South America. Size: 1.1-1.7 m (43-67 inches), including tail. Margays usually hunt at night for small mammals, birds and snakes. They're good at not being seen, either by their prey or by people. During the day, they sleep on a branch or in vegetation.

1. Begin by lightly drawing a titled oval. Add a triangle for one eye, and an oval shape with circle inside for the other.

2. Draw a triangle for the nose. Add the mouth, and facial markings. Spend some time with the face to get it right.

3. Add ears and more facial markings. Lightly draw the front leg, and a horizontal line for the chest.

4. Lightly sketch the other front leg and paw. Look carefully at the angles!

5. From the ear, draw the curving back, and the line on the bottom, curving into the rear leg.

   Now add the rear leg. Where do the lines connect to the body?

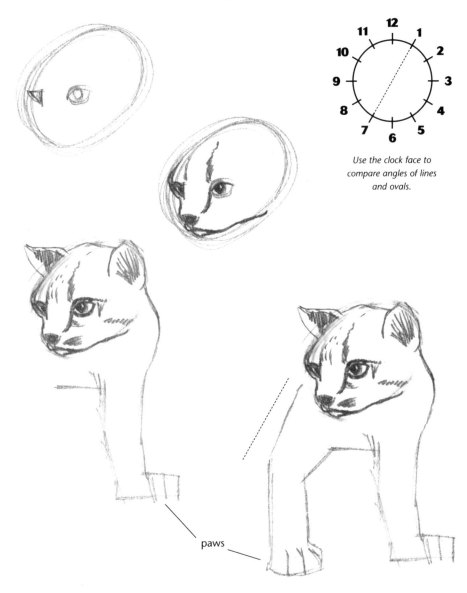

Use the clock face to compare angles of lines and ovals.

paws

Back

L**oo**K

Turn your drawing as you draw to avoid smudging it with your hand.

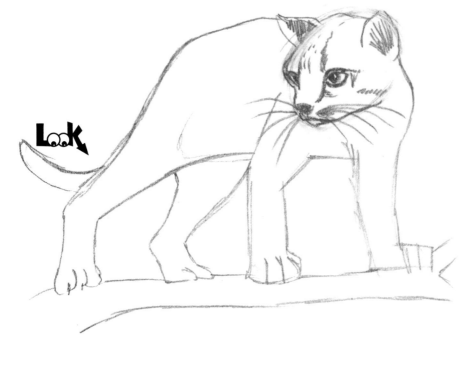

Loo**K**

6. Look how far back the other rear leg goes! Draw it. Add the tail – where does it connect? Draw whiskers, and a branch for the margay to stand on.

Last chance to fix the basic shapes of your cat! Look at it carefully – is everything OK?

Look at your drawing in a mirror (or through the back of the paper) to spot any areas you can make better.

7. Before drawing spots, look closely at this drawing. Notice how some spots curve to show the contour of the body. Which parts of the drawing are dark, and which are light? Is the tail as dark as the ears? What's the darkest part of the drawing?

Be patient as you finish the drawing. Work slowly and carefully as you add the spots.

Clean up any smudges with your eraser.

Magnificent Margay!

Okapi

Okapia johnstoni: Zaire.
Size: 1.5-2.3 m (5-7.5 ft).Lives alone except in breeding season. Long tongue – an okapi can clean its own eyes and eyelids with its tongue! Feeds on leaves, shoots, grass and fruit.

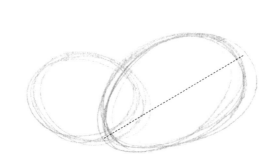

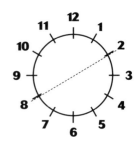

Use the clock face to compare angles of lines and ovals.

1. Start by drawing two light ovals for the body.

   Notice that
   • they overlap,
   • they're tilted and
   • they're different sizes.

2. Add the lines to join the two ovals top and bottom. Draw the neck, then very lightly add an oval for the main part of the head. Add the front of the head, with the mouth and eye.

3. Add the ear and small horns at the top of the head. Draw the rear leg and the front leg, looking closely at the angles in the drawing. Add the tail.

4. Carefully erase the the body ovals where they *overlap.* (You did draw them *lightly,* didn't you?) Lightly outline the distinctive stripes on the upper legs. Add the dark part on the lower legs. Draw some jagged lines for grass.

5. To complete your drawing, shade the body with pencil strokes showing the direction of the fur. Carefully erase the head oval, then add details and shade the head.

Take a good look at your drawing. Are there areas that need to be darker? Darken them. Are details getting fuzzy?

While your pencil is sharp, go over fine details. As it gets duller, add shading.

 Turn your drawing as you draw to avoid smudging it with your hand.

Clean up any smudges with your eraser.

Idea: the okapi looks like it's stretching to reach food. Add a branch with leaves on it. Draw the okapi's long tongue grabbing a leaf.

Orangutan

Pongo pygmaeus: Sumatra, Borneo. Size: 1.2-1.5 m (4-5 ft). The orangutan's arms are larger and stronger than its legs, and it is an agile climber. All adults have fatty throat pouches; only mature males have the distinctive cheek flaps surrounding the face. The shaggy fur is reddish-brown.

1. Draw the outline of the face, a tilted rectangle with a rounded bottom. Draw two lines near the middle of the rectangle for the mouth.

2. At the top of the rectangle, draw a series of curved lines to make the eyes. Draw two nostrils, and two lines to define the outside of the nose. Add radiating pencil strokes to make the 'beard.'

   Add hair at the top of the head. Lightly sketch the cheek flaps that surround the face. It may take you a try or two to get them just right.

3. Add the throat pouches, which look like a collar. Add shading to the face, cheek flaps and throat pouches.

4. Here's a big jump! *Draw lightly at first*, and redraw any parts that don't look right the first time. Draw an oval for the body. Add the legs, looking carefully at the position and the way the lines run. Add the outstretched arms, then draw the branch and vine for the orangutan to swing on.

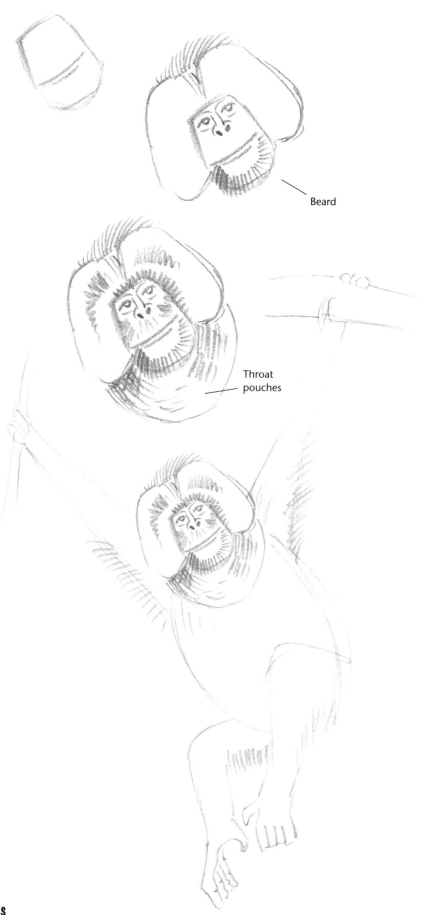

Beard

Throat pouches

5. Add another branch or two. Using short pencil strokes, draw the hair on the body. Pay close attention to the direction of the hair. Draw hair on arms and legs, pointing outward from the body. Add shading and texture to the branch and vine.

Notice areas that are darker and areas that are lighter. Go over any lines that need darkening.

While your pencil is sharp, go over fine details. As it gets duller, add shading.

 Turn your drawing as you draw to avoid smudging it with your hand.

Clean up any smudges with your eraser.

Idea: turn to pages 60-61, and fill the space around the orangutan with leaves, trees, and vines.

Ouakari

Cacajao calvus (bald ouakari): West Brazil. Size: 66-73 cm (26-29 inches) including tail. Lives in treetops. Bald head, red face and a beard! Walks on all fours; has a short tail and doesn't leap much. Eats mainly fruit. Active in the daytime.

1. Look carefully at the shapes in this drawing before you draw. Start with the branch, then add the banana-like oval of the body.

2. Add *(lightly!)* a second *overlapping* .oval for the top of the leg. Draw the bottom part of the leg, with toes curling around the branch.

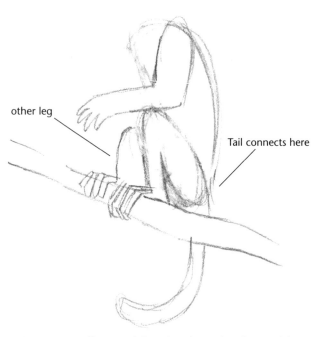

other leg

Tail connects here

3. Erase the first oval where the leg *overlaps* it. Draw the arm, with fingers.

4. Draw a small curved line for the other leg. Add toes. Draw the tail, starting from the base of the back.

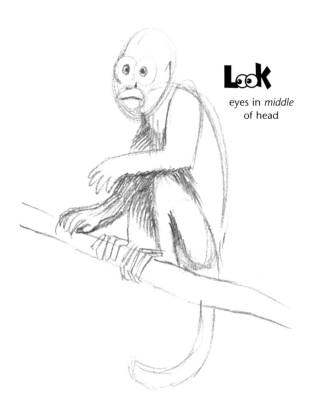

4. Add the second arm. Darken it with short pencil strokes for hair. Notice the direction of the hair.

5. Draw an oval for the head. In the middle, add two circles for the eyes, and an oval beneath them, with a line through the middle, for the mouth.

6. Carefully Shade the face and add long hair. Shade lightly at first! You can always make it darker.

6. Add lots and lots of hair! Make some areas darker. Use short pencil lines to make the back and tail look shaggy.

Draw Rainforest Animals **41**

Pangolin

Manis tricuspis (tree pangolin): Central Africa. Size: 84-105 cm (33-41 inches, including tail). Good climber with distinctive pointed scales. Feeds at night on ant and termite nests in trees, which it tears open with its sharp claws. Sleeps during the day in a tree, or in a hole it digs in the ground.

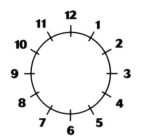

Use the clock face to compare angles of lines and ovals.

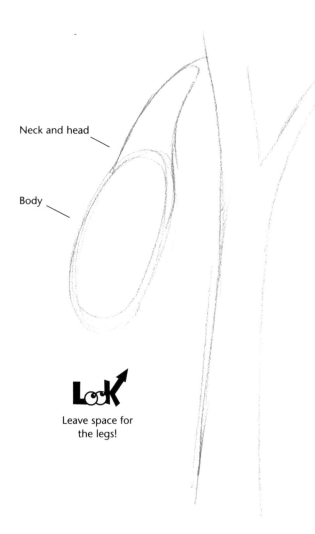

Neck and head

Body

Leave space for the legs!

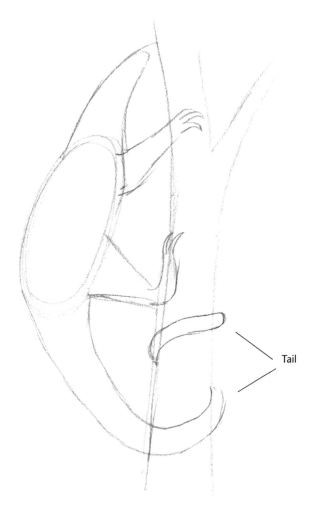

Tail

1. Lightly sketch the tree. Leaving room for the legs, draw a vertical, slightly tilted oval for the body. Draw a long curving shape for the neck and head.

2. Add the front leg, with its sharp claws. Draw the L-shaped rear leg. Extend the lower end of the oval to make the tail, curling around the tree.

 Turn your drawing as you draw to avoid smudging it with your hand.

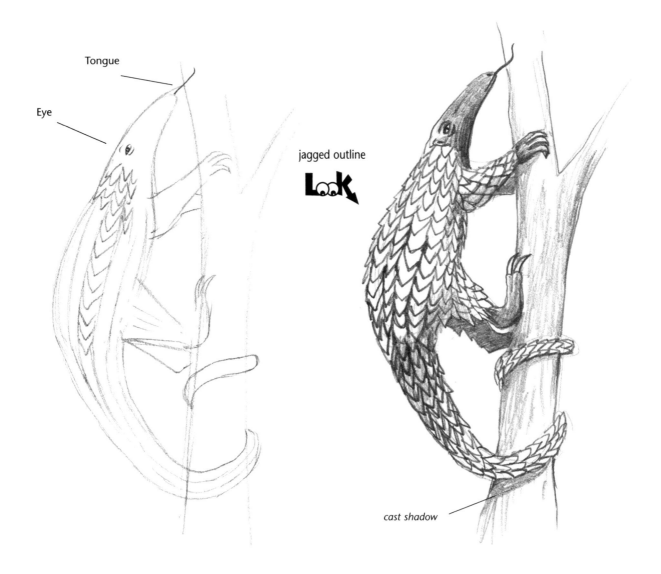

Tongue

Eye

jagged outline

LooK

cast shadow

3. Add the little bit you can see of the other two legs. Draw the long tongue (termites – yum!). Add the eye. Now you have the basic body parts in place. Next draw the scales. Start with light guide lines, like stripes, and draw little V shapes inside them.

4. Cover all but the face and feet with scales. Shade the head and feet, making the legs farthest away darker. Add some texture to the tree with light pencil strokes. Draw a little bit of *cast shadow* on the tree from the tail and legs.

Idea: add some termites on the tree for the pangolin to eat!

Quetzal

Pharomachrus mocinno: Mexico, Central America. Size: 30 cm (12 inches); tail feathers 61 cm (24 inches). Lives in lower layers of rainforest trees. Feeds on fruit and small animals like lizards and frogs. Long tail feathers, shed every year, were prized by the Maya, to whom the bird was sacred.

1. Start by drawing a light circle for the head. Add the eye and beak.

Use the clock face to compare angles of lines and ovals.

2. Make two short lines for the neck and back of the head, then draw a line for the front edge of each wing. Notice the direction each line points; think of a clock face.

3. Continue the lines of the head to form the body. Add curved lines for the inside part of each wing. Make light marks for spacing before drawing the feathers.

4. Draw the feathers.

5. Add feet and the main tail feathers. Draw short, radiating lines for feathers on the head. Darken the eye, leaving a white spot in it. Add more lines, in the center of each feather. Use short dark pencil strokes for feathers on the head, neck and breast.

Look!

feathers *radiate* outward

Tail feathers

Feet

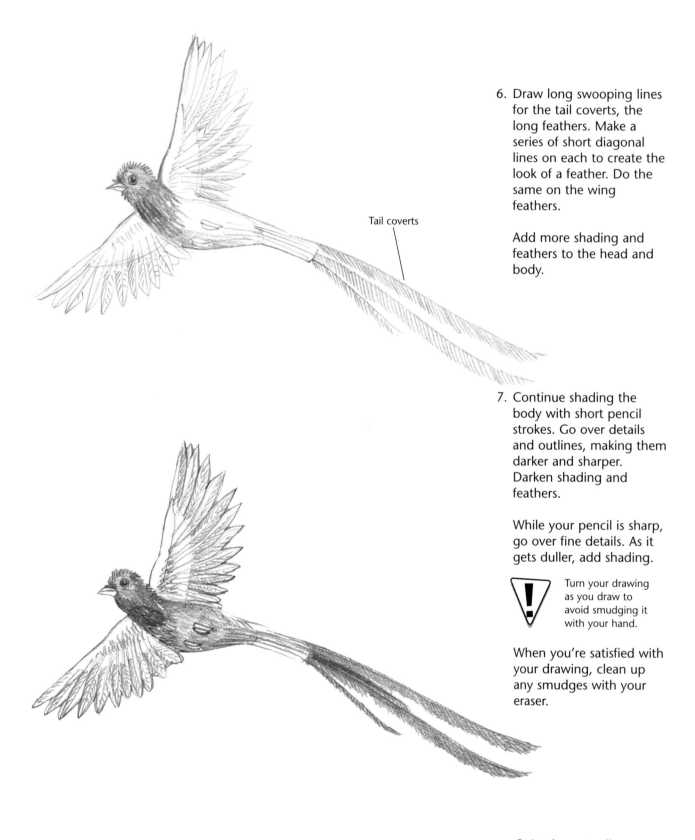

6. Draw long swooping lines for the tail coverts, the long feathers. Make a series of short diagonal lines on each to create the look of a feather. Do the same on the wing feathers.

Add more shading and feathers to the head and body.

Tail coverts

7. Continue shading the body with short pencil strokes. Go over details and outlines, making them darker and sharper. Darken shading and feathers.

While your pencil is sharp, go over fine details. As it gets duller, add shading.

⚠ Turn your drawing as you draw to avoid smudging it with your hand.

When you're satisfied with your drawing, clean up any smudges with your eraser.

Quite the quetzal!

Slender Loris

Loris tardigradus: Sri Lanka, southern India. Size: 18-25 cm (7-10 inches). Lives in trees, grasping carefully with its hands. Feeds at night; sleeps during the day in a tree, rolled up in a ball. To eat, it grabs insects (grasshoppers are a favorite), lizards, and small birds with its hands.

Always draw lightly at first!

L**oo**k!

leave space for legs!

1. Draw two lines for a branch. Make it interesting by adding a curve or two. Above the branch, lightly draw a rectangle.

Use the clock face to compare angles of lines and ovals.

2. Draw the front legs. The one closest to you has two parts. You only see part of the other leg.

L**oo**K

one leg *overlaps* the other

3. Add the rear legs. Notice that they bend opposite to the front legs. Lightly draw the foot.

Foot

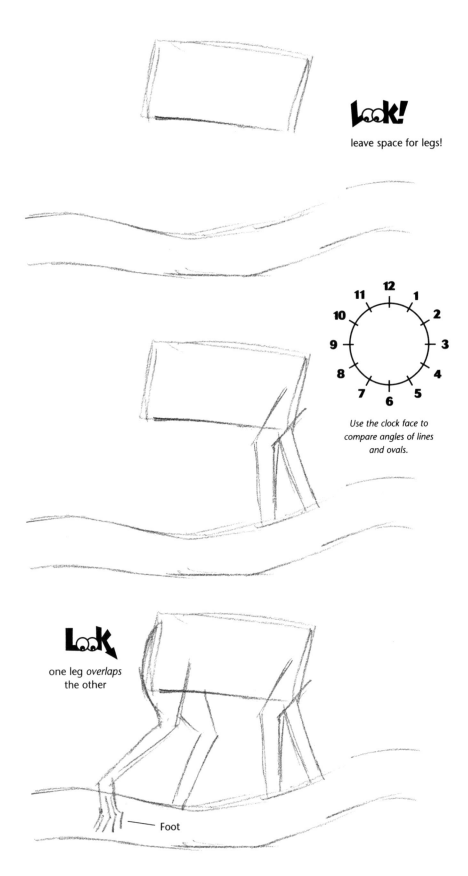

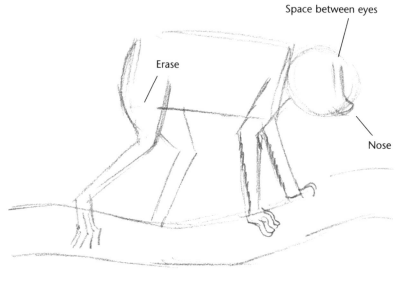

Space between eyes

Erase

Nose

4. Erase the rectangle where the rear leg *overlaps* it. Add the front feet. Lightly draw an oval for the head. Draw two lines to make the white space between the eyes. Add a bump for the nose.

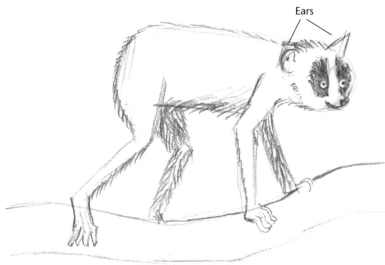

Ears

5. Darken the tip of the nose. Add mouth and eyes. Add dark areas around each eye. Draw the ears – one a triangle and one rounded. Add short pencil strokes for fur. Start with the darkest areas.

Turn your drawing as you draw to avoid smudging it with your hand.

6. Add fur to cover the whole body. Add texture and shading to the branch. Sharpen details such as the feet.

Clean up your drawing by erasing any smudges.

Idea: add epiphytes (see page 61) and other vegetation.

Sloth

Bradypus tridactylus: Central and South America. Size: 56-67 cm (20-26 in). Ve-ee-ee-ry slo-o-ow mo-oo-ving animal. Spends most of its life hanging upside down in trees. Eats leaves and tender buds.

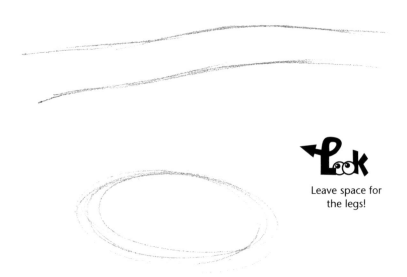

Leave space for the legs!

1. Draw two lines for the tree branch. Make it interesting by adding curves. Below the branch, draw an oval for the sloth's body

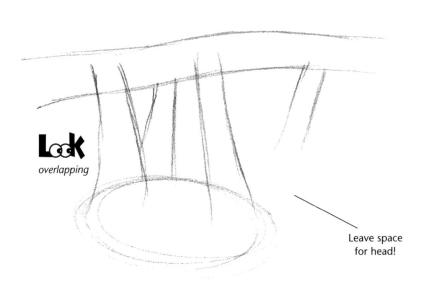

overlapping

Leave space for head!

2. Draw straight lines upward for the legs, at angles. Notice how one leg *overlaps* part of the one behind it. Draw just part of one front leg, to save space for the head.

3. Lightly draw a circle for the head. Where is it in relation to the body?

4. Add claws curving around the branch. Begin to add fur with short, downward strokes. The fur on a sloth grows this way because the sloth spends most of its life upside down!

5. Draw the face by starting with a small line for the mouth, at an angle, in the *center* of the circle. Add the nose, and the eyes just to the side of the nose. Draw dark fur areas extending from the eyes.

   Add short pencil strokes for the fur on the arms and legs, and on the back and neck.

6. Keep drawing short pencil lines to add fur to the rest of the body. Notice the areas that are darker, and the direction of the lines. Shade the tree branch. Fix any details you might have missed. Finally, clean up any smudges with your eraser.

Idea: add epiphytes (see p. 61) and other vegetation for this slo-o-ow sloth to hang out with.

Spider Monkey

Ateles paniscus (black spider monkey): Northern South America. Size: 1-1.4 m (39-55 inches). Tree dweller. Very agile, with a long reach and strong prehensile tail. Spider monkeys eat mostly fruit and nuts, and live in groups of 15-30.

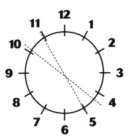

Use the clock face to compare angles of lines and ovals.

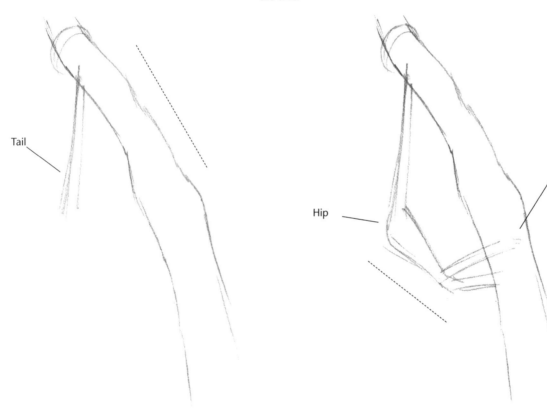

Tail

Hip

Closer leg

1. Draw the tree trunk, lightly. Make the lines interesting, not just straight!

   Draw two lines straight up for the tail. Then make the tail curling around the tree.

2. Add the hip and rear legs. The leg closer to you *overlaps* part of the one behind.

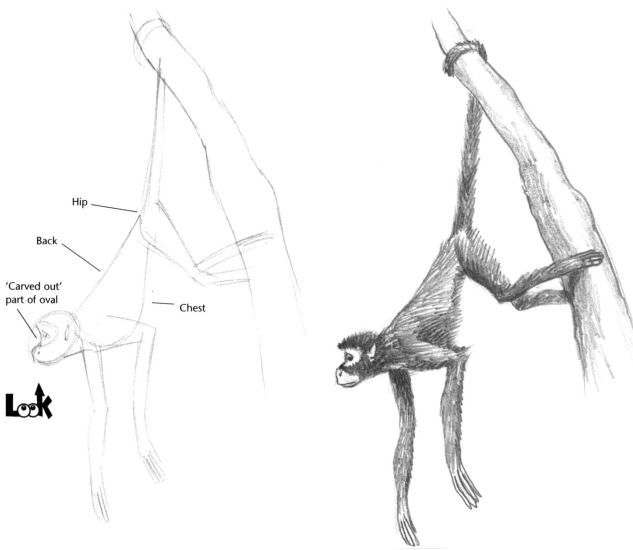

Turn your drawing as you draw to avoid smudging it with your hand.

Hip

Back

'Carved out' part of oval

Chest

3. From the hip, draw a straight line for the back, and a swooping curve for the chest.

Next, add long, spindly arms.

Lightly draw an oval for the head, then 'carve out' part of it to make the space above the nose. Draw the ear, eye, and nose. Draw a line to connect the head with the body.

4. With many short pencil strokes, add the fur. Notice the direction of the fur on different parts of the body. Also, notice that it's darker in some places.

Look for any lines that might need to be darkened. Add some shadows to the tree trunk. Clean up any smudges with your eraser.

Idea: this monkey looks like it's ready to reach for something, perhaps a vine or a branch…add vegetation to your drawing, including whatever the spider monkey is about to reach for.

Tamandua

Tamandua mexicana: Southern Mexico to South America. Size: 1.1 m (43 in) including tail. Tree-dwelling anteater with prehensile tail. Tears open nests with its strong claws, grabs ants and termites with its long, sticky tongue.

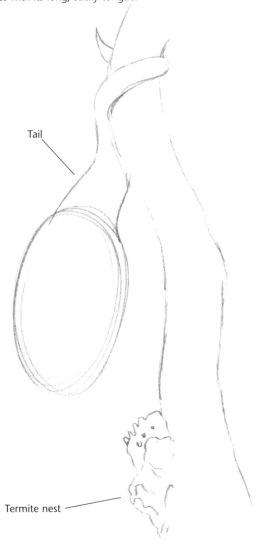

Tail

belly

Termite nest

1. Start by drawing an interesting tree trunk, which curves back and forth a little. At the bottom, draw a termite nest – it doesn't have to be fancy.

   Now draw an oval for the tamandua's body – *Draw lightly at first!* – and add the tail, curling up and around the tree.

2. Add the legs. Watch where they *overlap* each other. Draw lightly: remember, you can always make lines darker. Draw the sharp claws that the tamandua uses to tear open termite nests.

   Lightly erase parts of the oval where it *overlaps* the legs and tail. Make the belly curve inward between the front and rear legs.

Turn your drawing
as you draw to
avoid smudging it
with your hand.

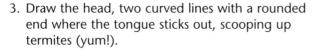

3. Draw the head, two curved lines with a rounded end where the tongue sticks out, scooping up termites (yum!).

Add the almond-shaped eye and the ears.

Look at the final drawing, noticing light and dark areas. Draw the dark fur with short pencil strokes.

4. Add more dark fur on the body. Leave the legs light. Draw shapes on the tree trunk to suggest peeling bark. Shade the tree trunk.

With a sharp pencil, sharpen any details that might be fuzzy – for example, the face or feet.

Use your eraser to clean up any smudges.

Extra bright idea: when you're finished, put your drawing on the wall where you can admire it the next time you and your friends are snacking on termites.

Tapir

Tapirus terrestris (Brazilian tapir): South America. Size: 2m (6.5 ft). Covered with short, bristly hair. Found near water (good swimmer). Feeds at night on leaves, buds, shoots, and small branches.

Always draw lightly at first!

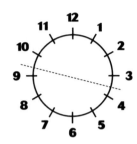

Use the clock face to compare angles of lines and ovals.

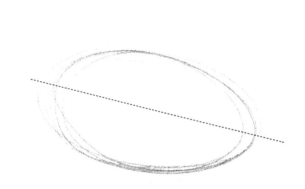

1. Drawing a tapir is quite easy. Start with a line for the ground, and above it, draw a slightly tilted oval.

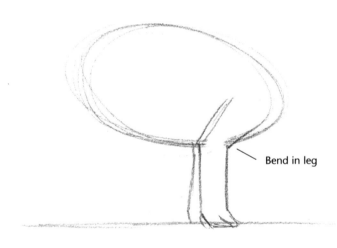

2. From the right side of the oval, draw the front leg with a bend in the middle, where it crosses the bottom of the oval. Erase the oval where the leg *overlaps* it. Draw the other front leg.

Bend in leg

3. Draw the short tail, and the back legs. Notice how and where these legs bend – well below the oval.

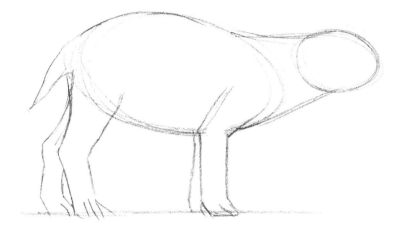

3. Lightly draw another oval for the head. Connect it to the body with two lines for the neck.

5. In the middle of the oval, draw an almond shape for the eye. Extend the top of the head to make the nose. From the nose, draw the mouth and the neck. Carefully erase what's left of the head oval.

Draw some leaves in the tapir's mouth. Add the short fur strokes above the eye. Draw the ears.

What a pretty face!

 Turn your drawing as you draw to avoid smudging it with your hand.

6. To finish your drawing, make many short pencil lines for the fur. Notice which places are dark, and which are light. Darken outlines in shadow areas, such as underneath the body. Add bristly marks on the outline of the back.

Add grass on the ground, and a bit of *cast shadow*, then clean up any smudges with your eraser and you're done!

Idea: add bushes and trees in the background.

Toucan

Ramphastos toco (Toco toucan): South America, mainly Amazon basin. Size: 61 cm (24 inches). Toucans eat a variety of fruits and large insects. Strong claws help them hang onto tree branches. Toucans grab food with their beak, then toss their head backwards to get it into their mouth.

Use the clock face to compare angles of lines and ovals.

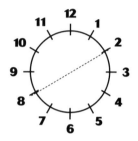

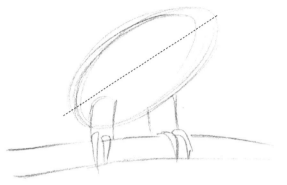

1. Draw the horizontal branch.

   Above it, at an angle, draw a titled oval, not quite touching the branch.

   Add vertical lines for the legs, with claws wrapping around the branch.

Shoulder

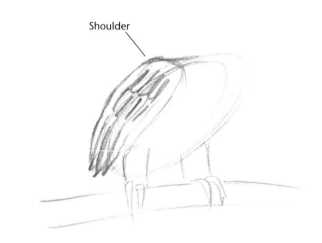

2. Add the wing, with a slight bulge at the shoulder.

   Draw lines on the wing to suggest feathers.

3. Extend the bottom of the oval for the tail. Draw the end of the tail behind and below the branch, with lines for feathers. Add small curved lines on the claws. Shade the leg.

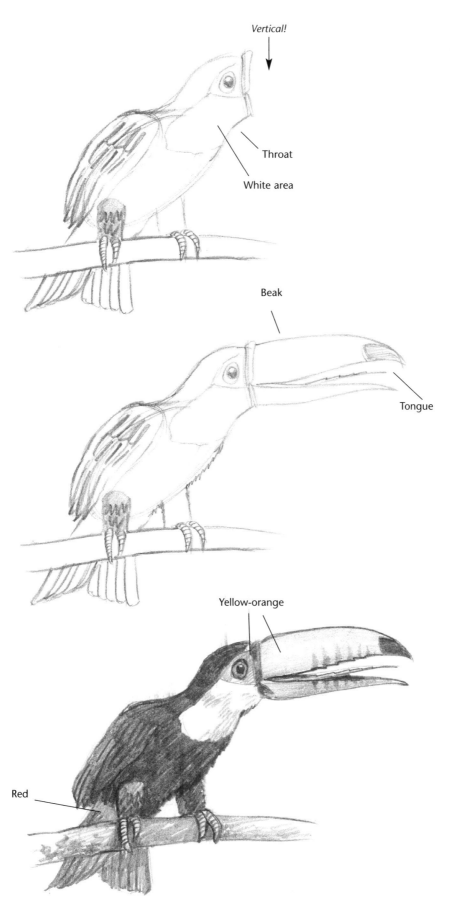

Vertical!

Throat

White area

Beak

Tongue

Yellow-orange

Red

4. Draw a line from the shoulder for the top of the head. Make the front of the head vertical where the beak attaches. Draw the throat. Add the eye, and the triangle around it. Outline the white area on the front of the body.

5. Now draw the beak – but first, look carefully at its curves. Make the top part of the beak wider than the bottom. Add the dark spot at the tip. Draw the tongue.

6. Look at the final drawing. Shade the dark areas of the bird. Add the pattern to the beak. Darken lines that seem important. Add shading to the branch.

While your pencil is sharp, go over fine details. As it gets duller, add shading.

⚠ Turn your drawing as you draw to avoid smudging it with your hand.

Look at your drawing in a mirror (or through the back of the paper) to spot any areas you can make better.

Clean up any smudges with your eraser.

Idea: draw a berry in the toucan's beak. Add color to your drawing…

Vine Snake

Oxybelis fulgidus: Central America and part of South America.
Size: 1.5-2 m (5-6.5 feet).
Slow-moving predator barely a half inch (1.25 cm) wide. Hard to see because it looks like a vine. Eats lizards and steals young birds from nests.

1. Start by drawing a thin branch with a few leaves. Your drawing doesn't have to look exactly like mine!

   Draw lightly at first!

2. Lightly sketch the outline of the snake. Make it curve this way and that. Position the snake's body so that it *overlaps* branches and leaves in several places. This drawing works best when the snake looks like it's slithering behind and in front of the branches.

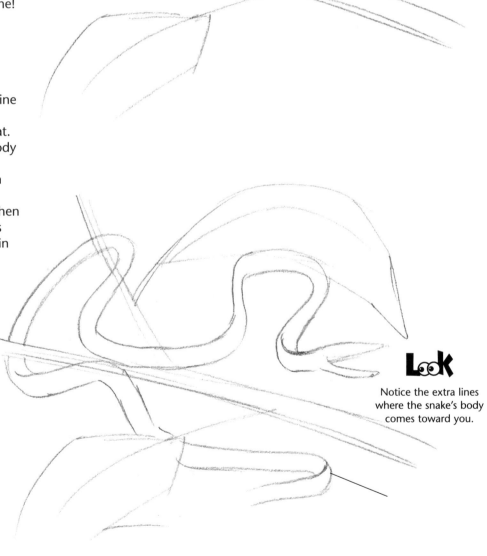

Look

Notice the extra lines where the snake's body comes toward you.

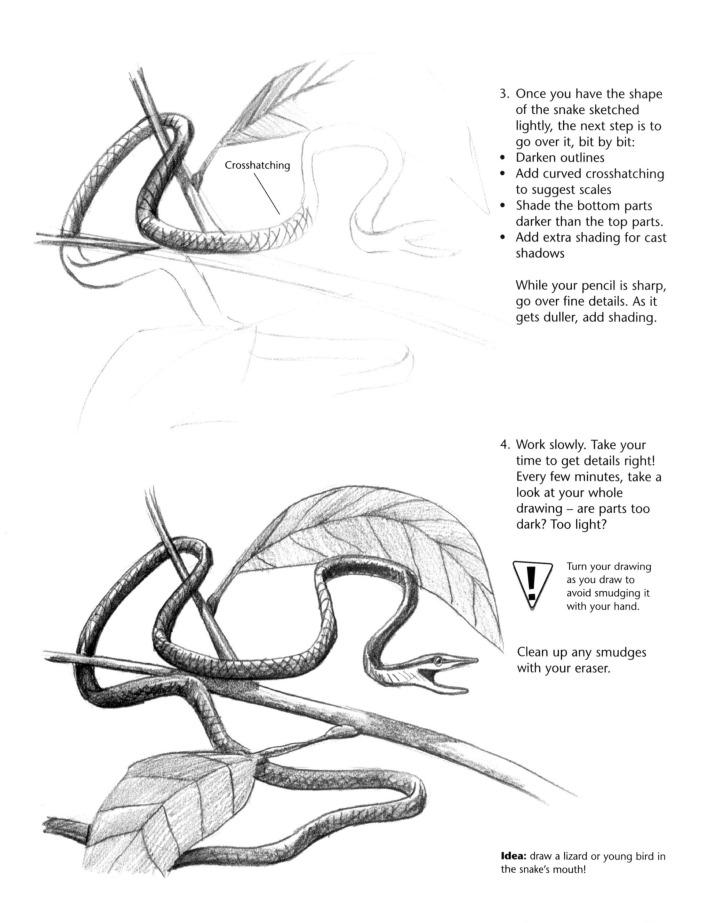

Crosshatching

3. Once you have the shape of the snake sketched lightly, the next step is to go over it, bit by bit:
   - Darken outlines
   - Add curved crosshatching to suggest scales
   - Shade the bottom parts darker than the top parts.
   - Add extra shading for cast shadows

   While your pencil is sharp, go over fine details. As it gets duller, add shading.

4. Work slowly. Take your time to get details right! Every few minutes, take a look at your whole drawing – are parts too dark? Too light?

   Turn your drawing as you draw to avoid smudging it with your hand.

   Clean up any smudges with your eraser.

Idea: draw a lizard or young bird in the snake's mouth!

Other ideas

When animals appear in the rainforest, chances are you won't see the whole animal because of the huge amount of vegetation all around them. To make your drawing more interesting, add foliage.

You'll find that it helps to draw the whole animal lightly, then draw the foreground elements, whether trees or leaves. Try not to cover up the most important parts of the drawing – for example, in the picture of the jaguar (right), I wouldn't want a leaf covering its face!

These two drawings are quick sketches – just a way of playing with ideas, to see what looks good and what doesn't. If I wanted to do a finished drawing of the howler monkey (below, right), I might do another sketch first, moving the leaves around to find a better arrangement.

The straight lines on the outside "crop" the drawing, to give a better idea how the finished drawing might appear.

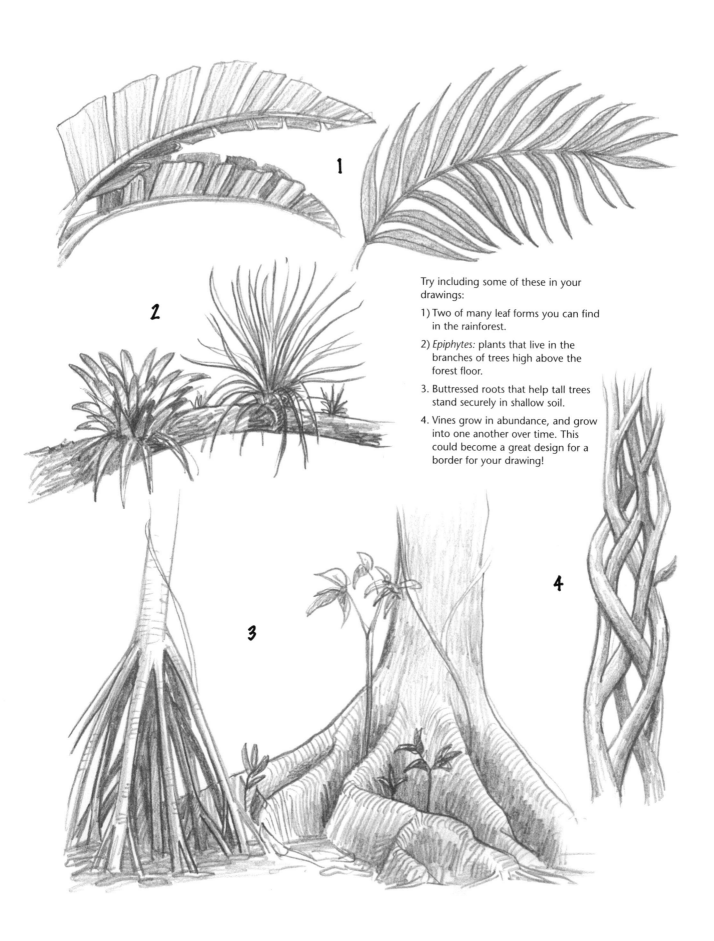

1

2

Try including some of these in your drawings:

1) Two of many leaf forms you can find in the rainforest.

2) *Epiphytes:* plants that live in the branches of trees high above the forest floor.

3. Buttressed roots that help tall trees stand securely in shallow soil.

4. Vines grow in abundance, and grow into one another over time. This could become a great design for a border for your drawing!

4

3

Save your work!

Whenever you do a drawing – or even a sketch – put your initials (or autograph!) and date on it. And save it. You don't have to save it until it turns yellow and crumbles to dust, but do keep your drawings, at least for several months. Sometimes, hiding in your portfolio, they will mysteriously improve! I've seen it happen often with my own drawings, especially the ones I knew were no good at all, but kept anyway....

Do-it-yourself portfolio

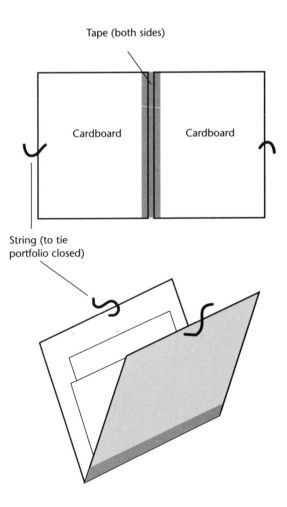

Tape (both sides)

Cardboard   Cardboard

String (to tie portfolio closed)

Index

Arrow Poison Frog 14

Basilisk Lizard.......................................6

Boa, Emerald Tree 10

Chimpanzee 8

Emerald Tree Boa.................................10

Flying Frog 15

Flying Squirrel 12

Frog, Arrow Poison 14

Frog, Flying 15

Frog, Tree 16

Gorilla 18

Hoatzin 20

Howler Monkey 22

Iguana 24

Jaguar..26

Kinkajou 28

Lemur (Ruffed) 30

Lizard, Basilisk......................................6

Loris 46

Macaw 32

Margay...34

Monkey, Howler 22

Okapi 36

Orangutan..38

Ouakari...40

Pangolin 42

Quetzal...44

Ruffed Lemur 30

Scarlet Macaw 32

Slender Loris..46

Sloth...48

Snake, Emerald Tree Boa.......................10

Snake, Vine 58

Spider Monkey 50

Squirrel, Flying 12

Tamandua 52

Tapir...54

Toucan 56

Tree Frog 16

Vine Snake...58

Learn about other books in
this series online at
www.drawbooks.com!